E. D.
Michael

WILD AND WONDERFUL:
The
WILDLIFE
of West Virginia

Q quarrier press

First Edition

10 9 8 7 6 5 4 3 2 1

Printed in China

Production Date   September, 2012
Plant & Location Printed by Everbest Printing (Guangzhou, China), Co. Ltd
Job / Batch #   110981

Library of Congress Control Number: 2012949683
ISBN-13: 978-1-891852-88-6
ISBN: 1-891852-88-4

Book & cover design: Mark S. Phillips

Distributed by:

West Virginia Book Company
1125 Central Avenue
Charleston, WV 25302
www.wvbookco.com

SNAIL

Most snail species are difficult to identify, unless one closely examines the shell, foot, and fleshy portions of the head. The land snail pictured here is one of several species found in West Virginia. Typically herbivorous, most snails have a rasp-like tongue that tears plant food into tiny pieces. Many land snails are nocturnal and trails of slime created to facilitate crawling are the best evidence of their presence.

ASIAN LADYBUG

The Asian ladybug is one of several exotic species that cause problems in West Virginia. Intentionally introduced throughout North America to control aphids and scale insects, this exotic is now widespread and common. Typically invading homes during October, this pest causes permanent stains and releases unpleasant odors when squashed. In addition it is inclined to bite. Native ladybugs may decline due to increased competition from this invader.

RED MILKWEED BEETLE

Milkweed flowers attract a variety of insects, one of which is the red milkweed beetle. Few insects, however, feed on milkweed leaves because of their poisonous nature. The milkweed beetles, similar to monarch butterfly caterpillars, acquire not only nourishment from milkweed leaves but also an unpleasant taste that protects them from predatory birds.

PRAYING MANTIS

The praying mantis is arguably the easiest insect to identify in West Virginia. Its size (nearly six inches long), its color (typically green), and its unique shape distinguish it from all other insects. And if more assistance is needed for identification, its behavior of holding the two prominent spiked forelegs in a praying position, for which it is named, convinces even the amateur entomologist. This carnivore feeds exclusively on living prey, primarily insects. Most are ambush feeders, patiently remaining motionless until prey approach too near. Extremely slow-moving and rarely flying, these ancient-looking insects are present in most flower gardens and farm fields. Although homeowners may not see the adult mantis, they frequently discover the tan, quarter-size egg capsules attached to small limbs of woody plants. Each of these capsules contains several hundred eggs, which hatch in spring after spending the winter in a dormant stage.

HONEY BEE

Honey bees are not native to West Virginia or North America, but were introduced by early European settlers. Although wild honey bees exist in most wooded areas the majority are raised commercially in beehives. In West Virginia, these bees produce over 400,000 pounds of honey each year, but they are more valuable as pollinators of cultivated crops. A single colony, which consists of workers, drones, and a single queen, may number as many as 40,000. Honey bee colonies throughout WV have declined in recent years due to mites, foulbrood, and mysterious colony collapse. Successful pollination of commercial crops, especially those in orchards, is at risk.

LUNA MOTH

The luna moth is one of the largest and most attractive moths found in West Virginia. With a wingspread over 4 inches, long tapering hind wings, and a striking lime green color, it is easily identified. Eyespots scattered over the wings serve to confuse potential predators. Luna moths are most commonly seen at night, thus the basis for their common name. Adult moths exist solely to mate and produce eggs (100-300). They do not eat and live only seven days. In contrast, luna moth caterpillars live 25-35 days and feed on a variety of trees, including birch, hickory, persimmon, and sumac.

MONARCH BUTTERFLY

Monarch butterflies have one of the most fascinating life cycles of any insect in West Virginia. Adults can be observed while they feed on milkweed flowers, and a close examination of the plants will reveal the yellow-and-black-banded larvae. Both caterpillars and adult butterflies are poisonous or distasteful to most birds and mammals because the caterpillars feed on milkweed. Monarch butterflies are the only butterfly that migrates north and south similar to birds, with large numbers of adults wintering in the mountains of Mexico.

CHANNEL CATFISH

Channel catfish exist in most rivers and lakes. Four pairs of barbels (whiskers) surround the mouth. These whiskers contain concentrated taste buds, which aid in finding food. A deeply forked tail and black spots (less obvious on older fish) distinguish it from the other catfish species that occur in West Virginia's waters. Larger adults reach a weight of 30 pounds and a length of 30 inches. Highest populations exist in deep waters with clean bottoms of sand or gravel and an absence of dense stands of vegetation.

DIANA

The diana is the most beautiful of all fritillary butterflies. Males, typically smaller than females, can be identified by their boldly-patterned orange and black wings. In contrast, females have dark blue or black wings with bright blue markings. Females scatter their eggs around violet plants, upon which the larval caterpillars typically feed. The word fritillary means checkered, and refers to the wing spots. Certain lily plants are also named fritillaries, in reference to their checkered leaves.

SMALLMOUTH BASS

The smallmouth bass resembles the largemouth bass, but in a smallmouth the posterior end of the upper jaw does not usually extend beyond the rear edge of the eye, and there is no dark lateral band extending along the side. Smallmouth bass require clearer, cooler waters than largemouths, and they frequent streams, rivers, and reservoirs with sandy bottoms. Primary foods of smallmouth bass are crayfish, minnows, and insects.

LARGEMOUTH BASS

Largemouth bass are the most sought-after fish in West Virginia. Present in nearly every stream, river, pond, lake, and reservoir, these game fish provide excellent fishing opportunities throughout the state. These bass are the primary target in most fishing derbies. Females, which are often larger than males, can reach a weight of 10 pounds and a length of 24 inches. Citation size fish in West Virginia must weigh five pounds and be 21 inches long.

BLACK CRAPPIE

Two species of crappie occur in West Virginia. The black crappie, shown here, resembles the white crappie, but has fewer dorsal spines and lacks the chain-like double bands on its back and sides. Black crappie commonly form large schools around weed beds and fallen trees where they feed on minnows, aquatic insects, and small fish. This is an angler favorite because of its abundance, ease of capture, and delicate flavor. A bluegill is in the background.

BROOK TROUT

The brook trout is, arguably, the most colorful of all West Virginia's game fishes. Its lower fins are orange-red with a white stripe on the leading edge. Equally striking, are the brilliant red spots encircled by blue haloes along its sides. It has a diverse diet, including insects, mollusks, crayfish, frogs, salamanders, and small fish. Optimum habitat for this trout consists of clean, cold, well-oxygenated mountain streams containing numerous pools. This, our only native trout, is officially recognized as West Virginia's State Fish.

RAINBOW TROUT

The rainbow trout is easily identified by a broad pink or red band along its sides and numerous small dark spots on its head and back. Originally restricted to the tributaries of the Pacific Ocean, from California to Alaska, it is the most widely transplanted of all game fish. Released in 45 countries and easily reared in hatcheries, these colorful trout are stocked annually in various streams, rivers, and lakes throughout West Virginia. They require cold water, however, so few survive the summer months.

GOLDEN TROUT

The golden trout is a color mutation of the rainbow trout. Discovered at a Petersburg fish hatchery in 1955, WVDNR hatcheries produced numerous brood stock through selective breeding. Named the West Virginia Centennial Golden Trout, to commemorate the state's 100th anniversary, these trout were first released in state waters in 1963. They are currently widely stocked throughout West Virginia and are a prize for most anglers.

BROWN TROUT

The brown trout is not native to West Virginia. It was introduced into North America from Europe in the 1880s. Many stockings were made in West Virginia's waters during the 1900s. This species, which feeds primarily on insects, can tolerate higher water temperatures than other trout. Brown trout have been associated with declines in native brook trout.

MUSKY

The muskellunge, or musky as it is commonly called, is the largest member of the pike family. A large mouth and numerous needle-like teeth make possible the capture of fish, snakes, frogs, ducklings, crayfish, or almost any living aquatic animal. Musky prefer clear water with weed beds and rock outcrops from which they can ambush their prey. This species may reach a weight of 40 pounds and a length of 50 inches.

LONGNOSE GAR

Longnose gar, or needlenose gar, are easily identified by their cylindrical shape, large diamond-shaped scales, and elongated snout with many teeth. Gar inhabit medium-to-large rivers with slow current, where they bask at the surface. Quite predaceous, the gar's diet includes mainly small fishes. A specialized air bladder, which functions as a lung, enables gar to breathe air and obtain oxygen. They do have functional gills and can obtain oxygen from the water like most fishes.

SPOTTED SALAMANDER

The spotted salamander inhabits most deciduous forests in West Virginia but is rarely seen due to being nocturnal and subterranean. Easily identified by its gray or black color and large yellow dorsal spots, this salamander may reach a length of eight inches. Breeding occurs on warm rainy nights during February and March in small pools where egg masses containing as many as 250 eggs are deposited.

EFT/NEWT

The eft is the terrestrial, sexually immature subadult of
the red-spotted newt, a small aquatic salamander. Newts,
considered the sexually mature adult phase, frequent ponds
and pools, especially those supporting wetland plants.
Female newts produce as many as 300 eggs, attaching each
to aquatic vegetation. After hatching, the larvae develop
gills and limbs and remain in the water until transforming
into the brightly colored red eft stage in late summer or
early fall. The slow-moving, brightly colored efts may be
seen moving across the forest floor throughout much of
West Virginia as they search for small invertebrates. After
several years as a land animal, efts return to water and
assume the greenish-brown adult coloration of a newt.

GRAY TREEFROG

The gray treefrog is one of two West Virginia treefrog species. Adhesive discs on the ends of their toes enable these two-inch frogs to move easily through trees in search of invertebrates such as ants, beetles, and spiders. Like most amphibians, gray treefrogs migrate in early spring to small bodies of water where females lay as many as 1,800 eggs.

BROAD-HEADED SKINK

The broad-headed skink, West Virginia's largest lizard, reaches a length of 12 inches. It spends most of its summer months in trees, searching for ants, insects, and spiders. Females typically deposit as many as 20 eggs in loose soil or under logs. Juveniles have a bright blue tail, similar to that of the five-lined skink. Broad-headed skinks have been collected in Cabell, Calhoun, Fayette, Jefferson, Kanawha, Logan, Nicholas, Tucker, and Wayne counties and probably inhabit several other counties. Other lizards found in West Virginia include the fence-lizard, six-lined racerunner, coal skink, five-lined skink, and little brown skink.

SPINY SOFTSHELL TURTLE

The spiny softshell is one of only two turtle species in West Virginia that does not possess a hard shell (the other is the smooth softshell). In addition to having a thin shell with flexible edges, this aquatic turtle is characterized by its elongated snout, with nostrils opening at the tip end. Common in many of the larger, slow-moving rivers, this turtle is rarely seen except when extending its nostrils out of the water to obtain oxygen. Similar to snapping turtles, female soft-shelled turtles leave the water to deposit their eggs in a sunny, sandy spot. A water strider also appears in the photograph.

BOX TURTLE

The box turtle is the only turtle native to West Virginia
that can totally withdraw its head, tail, and legs into
the protection of its ornately colored, hard shell. When
disturbed, by humans or potential predators, a box turtle
typically relies on the protection of its shell for defense. Box
turtles are the most terrestrial of all turtles in West Virginia.
This omnivore feeds on a variety of plant and animal
materials, including earthworms, crickets, slugs, snails,
blackberries, strawberries, and mushrooms. Males have red
eyes, whereas females have brown. Following mating the
female deposits 4-5 eggs in a flask-shaped hole and the
sun's warmth promotes incubation. Similar to most reptiles,
the young receive no parental assistance and must fend for
themselves following hatching.

RIBBONSNAKE

The ribbonsnake, shown here, closely resembles the gartersnake. Both species have three longitudinal stripes extending the length of the body. The ribbonsnake typically has bright yellow stripes on a rich brown background, whereas the background color of a gartersnake may be brown, blue, green, or red. Ribbonsnakes and gartersnakes often reach a length of 36 inches, with the slender tail comprising over one-third of the total length. While most snakes lay eggs, these both bear live young, typically 8-15. All non-venomous snakes in West Virginia, including the ribbon and garter, have a round eye pupil. In contrast, the pupils of venomous snakes (copperhead and rattlesnake) are elliptical or vertical.

COPPERHEAD

The copperhead is one of only two venomous snakes in West Virginia. Although not nearly so dangerous as rattlesnakes, the venom from a full-grown copperhead is lethal enough to kill young children and incapacitated adults. A healthy adult can typically survive a copperhead bite, but will endure significant pain. A copperhead will often vibrate its tail in dry leaves, producing a sound similar to that of a rattlesnake. The purpose is to warn large animals and humans of the snake's presence, and to prevent the snake from being stepped on.

RATTLESNAKE

The timber rattlesnake is the largest, most venomous snake in West Virginia. Dorsal color ranges from sulphur-yellow to black. Readily identified by their tail rattles, these large, thick-bodied snakes were once widely distributed throughout all counties. Individuals exceeding six feet in length were commonly reported in the 1800s. Due to collecting, slaughter, and habitat loss they are now relatively scarce. Winter dens, often attracting hundreds of rattlesnakes, are located on east-facing hillsides where ground temperatures are higher than the nearby forest.

CARDINAL

The cardinal, West Virginia's State Bird, is distinguished by the male's bold red plumage. Cardinals were rare in West Virginia when the state was covered with forests, but have adapted to landscaped lawns with their sunflower-laden feeders and are now present in most yards. Present year-round, this seedeater is well equipped for cracking open a sunflower seed and eating the kernel. Often one of the first birds to arrive at a feeder in the morning, cardinals are typically the last to eat prior to darkness settling over the neighborhood.

BLUEBIRD

The bluebird was historically not abundant in West Virginia, but with the advent of small farms during the 1800s bluebird numbers increased dramatically. Pastures and hayfields provided the insects vital to this colorful songbird's diet, and fence posts provided nesting cavities. The wide spread use of pesticides and the abandonment of numerous farms in the mid-1900s led to a drastic decline in bluebird numbers. Nest box initiatives have led to a rebound in numbers.

EASTERN MEADOWLARK

The eastern meadowlark prefers grassy hayfields and
pastures where it can often be seen perched upon a
fencepost or small snag. Although the back
and sides are mottled brown, a black "V"
on a bright yellow breast makes identification
easy. This grassland bird nests directly on the ground
in a shallow depression lined with a few feathers and
dried grasses.

MALLARD

The mallard is the most familiar species of waterfowl in West Virginia. These year-round residents inhabit ponds, lakes, rivers, and marshes plus golf courses and city parks. The drab, brownish-colored female resembles many other dabbling ducks. By contrast, a male mallard is readily identified by its glossy green head, prominent white neck ring, and rich chestnut chest. Females are more vociferous than males, emitting loud "quacks" compared to the male's soft "kweks."

WILD TURKEY

Wild Turkeys exhibit the most spectacular breeding displays of any bird in West Virginia. A gobbler has the ability to transform its appearance almost instantly by changing colors of head and neck, fanning its tail feathers, puffing out its breast, dragging its wing tips along the ground, and enlarging the snood, a fleshy projection over the beak. Such dramatic performances are designed to impress male competitors and potential female mates. Following mating, the hen deposits 8-15 eggs at the rate of one per day in a shallow depression on the forest floor, often adjacent to a tree trunk or fallen log. Unlike the adults, which typically feed on acorns, grapes, berries, and other plant foods, young poults feed solely on invertebrates during their first 60 days of life. These precocial young are not fed by the female, but must find and capture everything they eat. Of no little importance to poult survival, the hen does provide protection during inclement weather.

RUFFED GROUSE

The ruffed grouse is named for the ruff of feathers that are prominent on males during the spring mating season. To announce his presence to competing males and potential mates, the male extends his neck ruff, erects his crest, puffs out his breast feathers, fans his tail feathers, and struts back and forth on a fallen tree trunk. The males, or cock birds, supplement their gaudy appearance by drumming with their wings. The mysterious drumming sound, which is created by rapid wing beats creating a vacuum into which air rushes, somewhat resembles a miniature sonic boom. Although it is rare to sight a drumming male, the drumming can be heard throughout most wooded habitats in West Virginia every spring. Ruffed grouse exhibit two color phases, the gray and the brown, with the latter being much more prevalent throughout West Virginia. Ruffed grouse feed on a variety of plant foods, including acorns, grapes, black cherries, viburnum fruits, tree buds, and fern tips.

GREAT BLUE HERON

The great blue heron is West Virginia's tallest bird. Standing over four feet tall, this long-legged bird wades through shallow waters in search of fish, frogs, snakes, crayfish, or other aquatic foods. Common to almost every river and lake during summer months, these birds seldom nest in West Virginia. In those rare sites where nesting does occur, several dozen nests will be clustered in tops of large trees alongside a river.

GREEN HERON

The green heron, or green-backed heron, is the smallest heron frequenting the waters of West Virginia. Present in every county, this heron typically perches in trees alongside a stream, river, or lake in search of small fish. Upon spotting its prey, the heron dives into the water and grasps the fish in its beak. After returning to a tree, the fish is swallowed whole. This bird was referred to as "fly-up-the-creek" or "shite-poke" before the days of bird books.

GREAT WHITE EGRET

The great egret, also named the common egret and American egret, is similar in appearance to the great blue heron, but is slightly smaller and less abundant in West Virginia. The common egret can be seen around edges of ponds, lakes, and rivers throughout the state during summer months. The sexes are similar in appearance, and have delicate ornamental feathers on their backs during breeding season. Winters are spent in warmer climates where aquatic foods are readily available.

PILEATED WOODPECKER

The pileated woodpecker is the largest of seven species of woodpeckers found in West Virginia. With a wingspan of nearly two feet, striking black and white plumage, and bright red feathers on its head, it is easily identified. This woodpecker hammers out large rectangular openings when searching for carpenter ants, its favorite food. Pileated woodpeckers tap on trees to determine which ones are hollow and then listen for the sounds made by ants, beetle larvae, and other insects, before chiseling an opening into the tree to obtain a meal.

CROW

The American crow is abundant and easily recognized throughout West Virginia. Only the raven is similar in appearance, but it has a heavier bill and a wedge shaped tail. Once restricted to agricultural areas where they caused considerable crop damage, crows now frequent towns and cities. Communal roosts, typically in conifers, attract thousands of crows every winter night.

BARRED OWL

The barred owl is the second largest owl found in West Virginia, exceeded only by the great-horned. Similar to most owls, females are larger than males. This species, named for the prominent transverse barring across its neck and upper breast, typically lives in areas containing dense stands of conifers such as pine, hemlock, or spruce. The "eight-hooter," as it is often labeled, produces a distinctive call consisting of eight wild notes, "hoo, hoo, hoo-hoo…hoo, hoo, hoo-hoo." Typically the call ends with a downward pitch. Because of small, relatively weak talons, barred owls generally hunt small prey such as frogs, crayfish, small birds, and small mammals. Barred owls typically sit in wait for their prey high in trees, rotating their necks as much as 270 degrees.

SCREECH OWL

The screech owl is the most abundant owl in West Virginia. However, being a nocturnal bird, it is rarely seen by humans. Its presence is revealed by its call, which can best be described as a low-pitched, quavering wail or whinny, rather than a high-pitched screech. Screech owls exhibit two distinct color phases, the gray and the red. A clutch of young will often contain both gray and red individuals. This is the second smallest owl in West Virginia, only the saw-whet owl being smaller. Screech owls occur in all wooded areas, including parks within cities. They nest in hollow trees, often in old woodpecker holes, where the female will lay 3-5 white eggs. Common foods of screech owls include mice, small birds, crayfish, small snakes, and large insects such as katydids.

GREAT HORNED OWL

The great horned owl is the largest owl native to West Virginia. With a wingspan of up to 50 inches and a height of 18-25 inches, these avian predators are capable of killing rabbits, skunks, raccoons, and young turkeys. This owl can be readily identified by its prominent feather tufts, which somewhat resemble ears. These year-round residents prefer wooded areas characterized by numerous grassy openings where rabbits are common. The call may best be described as deep resonate hooting (4-5 by males and 6-8 by females). Great horned owl nests are often located in old crow nests or hawk nests, rarely in tree cavities. Here, with the 2-3 white eggs exposed to the elements, it is necessary for the parents to provide warmth and protection. Because the eggs are typically laid in February, the incubating parent is often covered with snow during the 12 weeks when the young cannot fly.

BARN OWL

The barn owl, or monkey-faced owl as it is often named, was once one of the most abundant owls in West Virginia. During the 1800s, when small farms dotted much of the landscape, barn owls lived and nested in many barns. The abundance of mice, both within the barns and throughout the farm fields, provided the prey base upon which these helpful predators depended. With the demise of small farms and widespread use of pesticides, however, barn owl numbers plummeted.

TURKEY VULTURE

The turkey vulture is classified as a bird of prey, but does not kill its food. It is a scavenger, feeding on the carcasses of dead animals. With a wingspan of nearly 6 feet, these large birds are capable of soaring effortlessly for hours at a time. It can be easily distinguished from hawks and eagles by its naked red head and absence of flapping when flying. Turkey vultures often roost together at night in groups of over 200 individuals.

OSPREY

Osprey rarely nested in West Virginia prior to the 1900s, although they were common visitors during periods when water bodies were not ice-covered. Only six nests were documented prior to 1975. The WVDNR initiated a successful release program during the 1980s, transplanting young from Maryland to West Virginia. Osprey, also called fish hawks, currently nest in six West Virginia counties. These fish eaters detect their prey while flying and hovering, then dive and grasp the potential meal with their sharp talons. Most osprey spend winter months in Mexico, Central America, or South America.

PEREGRINE FALCON

Historically, peregrine falcons were widespread throughout North America until their populations declined drastically during the mid-1900s. These raptors were considered extirpated in West Virginia by 1970. Captive breeding and subsequent reintroductions have increased populations in West Virginia (i.e. New River Gorge) and eastern United States where they typically nest directly on cliff ledges and lay 3-4 eggs. Reputedly the fastest bird on earth, these fascinating predators reach over 200 mph during hunting dives.

BALD EAGLE

Bald eagles are only recent residents of West Virginia, probably due to the historic scarcity of open bodies of water where they could obtain their most common food, fish. The first known pair of nesting bald eagles within the mountain state was discovered in 1981 on the South Branch of the Potomac. Recent surveys indicate that as many as 11 pairs currently nest within West Virginia, with nest sites in Grant, Hardy, Hampshire, Pendleton, and Mineral counties. Bald eagles have made a dramatic comeback since the early-mid 1900s when there was doubt whether the species would survive. Once listed as endangered by the U.S. Fish and Wildlife Service, the species was downlisted to threatened in 1995, and removed from the threatened/endangered list in 2007. It is not unusual to spot these birds soaring over large lakes and rivers in West Virginia, especially during spring months. Adults develop the distinctive white head and white tail after five years.

OPOSSUM

The opossum is the only marsupial native to North America. Females have a pouch in which the newly born young complete their fetal development. Each pouch typically contains 13 teats, to which the young attach solidly until development is completed. Gestation is only 13 days, but young remain in their mother's pouch for two months. If more than 13 young are born the surplus do not survive. Opossums are true omnivores, eating plant or animal material, alive or dead. Adept tree-climbers, these 10-12 pound marsupials have a prehensile tail by which they can hang from tree limbs.

HAIRY-TAILED MOLE

The hairy-tailed mole is one of three species of moles found in West Virginia, the other two being the eastern mole and the star-nosed mole. A mole can be easily identified by its broad front feet, pointed nose, apparent lack of eyes and ears, and soft gray fur. This 4-5 inch long insectivore spends most of its life underground, where it feeds on a variety of insects and earthworms. Active both day and night, these subterranean mammals often consume three times their weight in 24 hours. The mounds of earth pushed to the surface while excavating underground tunnels cause unsightly problems in lawns and golf courses.

CHIPMUNK

Chipmunks prefer oak forests with numerous downed logs, but are equally abundant around bird feeders containing sunflower seeds. Seen mostly on the ground, they readily climb trees to gather fruits or nuts. Their sharp chuck-chuck-chuck call is most frequently heard during sunny October days. Underground dens protect against predators and inclement weather, and provide a secure nursery for litters of 2-8 youngsters.

GROUNDHOG

The groundhog, also known as woodchuck, marmot, or whistle pig, is the second largest rodent in West Virginia; only the beaver is larger. Weighing 5-10 pounds as adults, these vegetarians frequent grassy fields where they feed on succulent clovers, grasses, and a variety of herbaceous forbs. They can also be seen along paved highways where they eat salt spread to prevent icing. Groundhogs utilize a deep, extensive underground den system to raise their 2-6 young, avoid predators, and hibernate during winter months when herbaceous foods are unavailable. Groundhogs can cause considerable damage to crops, especially in gardens.

NORTHERN FLYING SQUIRREL

The northern flying squirrel is one of two species of flying squirrels found in West Virginia. The other, the southern flying squirrel, inhabits every county in the state. The West Virginia northern flying squirrel is listed as an endangered species by the U. S. Fish and Wildlife Service. It is restricted to seven counties: Grant, Greenbrier, Pendleton, Pocahontas, Randolph, Tucker, and Webster. Whereas southern flying squirrels commonly eat acorns, northern flying squirrels typically eat fungi and lichens.

GRAY SQUIRREL

The gray squirrel, one of the most widely distributed mammals in West Virginia, inhabits forests, woodlots, and city parks. These bushy-tailed rodents are usually gray, although black squirrels (a melanistic color phase) are present in many counties. Most common where mature oak trees abound, gray squirrels have learned to supplement their diets with sunflower seeds at backyard feeders. During the 1800s, these arboreal mammals emigrated across the Ohio River in numbers so large they sank small boats.

FOX SQUIRREL

Fox squirrels in West Virginia are typically rusty orange color, with pale yellow or orange belly hair. Slightly larger than gray squirrels, fox squirrels frequent open woodlots rather than dense forests. Walnuts are especially desired, but other kinds of nuts are also eaten. An adult fox squirrel can weigh up to three pounds.

BEAVER

The beaver is the largest furbearer in West Virginia,
reaching a weight of 60 pounds. These aquatic mammals
can modify their environment more than any other animal.
By building a dam they convert a small stream with steady
flowing water into a pond with still water. Stream plants
and animals are replaced by entirely different species. The
converted trout stream thus becomes home to bluegill and
bass. Green frogs, newts, cattails, and pondweeds become
established where none previously existed.

COTTONTAIL

The eastern cottontail and the New England cottontail are the only rabbit species found in West Virginia. Whereas eastern cottontails are found throughout West Virginia, the New England cottontail is restricted to mountainous areas. Nearly impossible to identify at a distance, the eastern cottontail has a rusty patch behind the ears that is lacking in the New England cottontail. Eastern cottontails produce 3-4 litters per year, with 4-7 young per litter. Young are born naked and blind, in a shallow depression in the ground.

WHITE-TAILED DEER FAWN

White-tailed deer fawns are typically born in May and June. While twins are common, does in excellent condition will produce triplets. Weighing 5-6 pounds at birth, and capable of wobbly walking, fawns spend their first few days of life secluded in dense vegetation, nursing several times each day when the mother returns. At 10 days of age they begin to eat vegetation, and can escape most predators. Most stop nursing at 2 months of age and lose their spots at 3-4 months of age.

WHITE-TAILED DEER

The white-tailed deer has exhibited extraordinary population swings during the last 200 years. Abundant in the 1700s, their numbers plummeted in the 1800s until fewer than 1,000 remained in West Virginia. With restrictions on hunting, abandonment of farms, and regrowth of forests, deer numbers began an unbelievable explosion. West Virginia now has over one million deer and their overall economic value is subject to considerable debate.

ELK

Elk were fairly common and widespread throughout West Virginia in the early 1700s. With the arrival of European trappers, settlers, and the extremely accurate muzzleloading rifle, however, their numbers declined precipitously. They were considered extirpated in West Virginia by 1880. In recent years, however, a few wild individuals have wandered into the state from Kentucky.

WILD BOAR

The non-native wild boar was introduced into West Virginia by the WVDNR in the 1970s, and is now concentrated in Boone, Logan, Raleigh, and Wyoming counties. During fall, boars feed primarily on acorns. At other times of the year, they consume fruits, nuts, tubers, grasses, insects, amphibians, salamanders, snakes, and bird eggs. At 400 pounds, males weigh nearly twice as much as females. Wild boars have the potential to cause major damage to agricultural crops, but fortunately have not significantly expanded their range.

RIVER OTTER

The river otter is one of the most entertaining mammals a person can have the good fortune to observe. This large member of the weasel family often exhibits an unusual curiosity towards humans. Otters eat a variety of wetland foods, including fish, turtles, frogs, crayfish, and mussels. Their valuable fur led to near extirpation by 1900, but reintroductions during the 1980s and 1990s by the WVDNR led to a healthy recovery of this fascinating furbearer. River otters now live in all major watersheds and most counties in West Virginia.

RACCOON

The raccoon can be readily identified by its ringed tail and masked face. This 20-pound omnivore has adapted to humans better than any other native mammal. Gardens, garbage cans, bowls of cat and dog food, and bird feeders, plus sewers and chimneys now characterize prime raccoon habitat. Unusual strength, agility, and dexterous front toes enable raccoons to survive in a city environment. Unfortunately, this proximity to humans has greatly increased the likelihood of raccoons biting humans and their pets, and introducing the deadly rabies virus.

STRIPED SKUNK

The striped skunk is one of two species of skunks existing in West Virginia. The other is the spotted skunk. Striped skunks are primarily carnivorous, feeding on earthworms, grubs, insects, mice, and bird eggs. They do not hibernate and become inactive during winter months. Small cat-like tracks meandering across the snow in February are evidence their winter dormancy has ended and breeding is underway. Skunks often share underground burrows with groundhogs, raccoons, and opossums, although not necessarily in close proximity.

BLACK BEAR

The black bear, West Virginia's State Mammal, is an omnivore that weighs as much as 600 pounds. Acorns dominate their diet, but they consume prey as small as ant eggs. Apples, beechnuts, grapes, serviceberries, skunk cabbage, grass, honey, yellow jacket larvae, and deer fawns are also consumed. Common in the 1700s, their numbers had declined so far by the early 1900s that some biologists believed they would be eliminated from the West Virginia landscape. Surprisingly, bears demonstrated an amazing ability to adapt to humans. By the year 2000, management was designed to reduce bear numbers rather than increase.

GRAY FOX

The gray fox has a salt-and-pepper colored coat with a
black stripe running atop a bushy, reddish gray tail. Often
difficult to distinguish from a red fox, call it a gray fox if you
are uncertain. Gray foxes, which frequently climb trees, are
more arboreal than red foxes. Primarily carnivores, gray
foxes also eat acorns, fruits, insects, and bird eggs. Similar
to most carnivores, gray foxes typically have only one
litter per year. An underground den or hollow log provides
protection for 3-7 pups born during April or May.

RED FOX

The red fox has a reddish-yellow coat, black feet, and white tip on a bushy tail. Its preferred habitat is brushy, overgrown fields with a high population of mice and rabbits. Controversy exists over whether the red fox is native to North America. Some biologists believe the red fox was introduced from England for the purpose of conducting English-style foxhunts with hounds and horses. Thousands of red foxes were indeed introduced from England, but low numbers of native red foxes may have existed in North America prior to these importations.

FISHER

The fisher, formerly known as the black fox, is a member
of the weasel family. This 10-pound carnivore preys on a
variety of mammals and birds, including mice, chipmunks,
rabbits, groundhogs, deer fawns, grouse, and wild turkey.
Once widespread throughout West Virginia, it had become
extirpated by 1900 due to excessive trapping and reduction
of available foods. Beginning in the 1970s, however, the
WVDNR reintroduced fishers into suitable mountainous
habitats. The program was a success and fishers are now
thought to inhabit at least 22 counties.

COYOTE

Historically, coyotes did not exist in West Virginia, or in any of the eastern United States. Currently, they are in every county in West Virginia. Restricted to Texas and the southwestern U. S. during the 1800s, the coyote began a steady and dramatic range expansion in the 1900s. The coyote now occurs throughout the eastern United States and Canada. It has been hypothesized that the range of the coyote was restricted by the presence of the timber wolf, through competition and direct predation. But with the extermination of the wolf from much of the United States by 1900, the coyote faced no serious competition and had no major predators. The dramatic increase of white-tailed deer provided a major food source for coyotes and undoubtedly contributed to their expansion. In addition to deer fawns, coyotes feed on a wide range of animals plus considerable plant matter. Although they kill many rodents they also occasionally kill sheep and calves.

BOBCAT

Bobcats are more common throughout West Virginia than most people realize. Their secretive nocturnal behavior and reluctance to cross paved roads reduce opportunities to see them. Present in every county, bobcats frequent wooded areas with abundant rodents, rabbits, and birds. Bobcats belong to the same family as mountain lions (*Felidae*), but are easily distinguished by their smaller size (15-30 pounds) and their short tail (3-4 inches).

MOUNTAIN LION

Mountain lions were once common throughout West Virginia. However, by the late 1800s they had been extirpated from much of the State. Although individual mountain lions may currently inhabit West Virginia, it is doubtful that a breeding population exists. Individuals currently roaming the mountains were most likely released from captivity by well-intentioned humans. Mountain lions are also known as cougars, panthers, and catamounts. These large cats primarily prey on white-tailed deer, although they have been known to eat various birds and mammals, plus domestic livestock. Being solitary hunters, they often wait motionless to ambush their prey. Adult males weigh as much as 200 pounds, while adult females weigh 100 pounds. A mountain lion's tail is almost 3 feet long and has a dark brown tip.

GRAY WOLF

Gray wolves, or timber wolves, were common throughout West Virginia prior to the 1800s, when an abundant prey base of deer, elk, and buffalo was available. Shooting, trapping, poisoning, and rabies, coupled with a shortage of large hoofed prey animals, led to their decline and eventual extirpation. The death of the last recorded wild gray wolf in West Virginia occurred around 1900.